I0584816

GOD TALK OF THE GORGE

ALASKA POEMS

ERIC GORDON JOHNSON

Cirque Press

Sandra Kleven — Michael Burwell
3157 Bettles Bay Loop
Anchorage, AK 99515

cirquejournal@gmail.com
www.cirquejournal.com

Cover art by Kay Haneline
Author photos by Cynthia Steele
Book Design by Lizzie Newell

Print ISBN:

979-8-9941916-0-6

Dedicated to

Gail Bakken Johnson and Marilyn Lee

Contents

Renewal

Growing Up In the Great Land

Baxter Bog, 1955

Below zero we cleared snow
and skated on black ice that cracked and moaned.
Methane bubbles hung suspended below our blades,
snickering and carving the surface to sugar.
No houses stood to see us
Only a few black dwarf swamp spruce.

Summertime we slogged over tussocks, sometimes
catching sight of trumpeter swans landing, legs stretched forward,
with white ungainly wings backpedaling furiously.
Stripped to our underwear we dove into the icy water,
only the top two feet warmed by the sun.

We swam down under the moss and sedges
that jutted out from shore, forming a watery cave.
Roots hung down in the frigid darkness
as our legs scissored and slithered the oozing peat below.
On shore again and pulling our pants over
white goose-pimpled thighs, we ran home
to Mother who panicked at what we had done.

They never found the Cessna that sank in the sonar-sucking muck.
There is no bottom's bottom to Baxter Bog.

Snow Trap

Snowsuit stuffed, I jump
from the trailer door into
new night-fallen snow, stuck

to my chest, frantically flailing
at nothing there is to
mitten grab hold of

unable to free my foot
caught by snow's old crust
buried below, my tears

freezing lashes shut,
madly shoving snow from
down along my leg. My

foot still fixed, Mother
tugs me up from the
clutches of the snow.

A Missed Connection

An eagle surveys from a cottonwood tree
the pond, geese pair and brood.

Sliding down the snowy hill, I smash
my forehead into a waiting sled.

Diving and swooping,
the great bird dips its talons.

Blood sprays on the snow as
I run for Mother, holding my forehead.

The gander rises up, swatting and squawking,
Mother goose nestles goslings under wing.

My mother misreads what happened,
strides past, bawling out Theresa and Mary.

Tiring, the wide-winged bird sails south.
and I, embarrassed, slink home.

It wasn't until after she passed away
I understood.

Running Mount Marathon

An Alaskan 5-kilometer race up and down 3,000 feet

Lined up at the starting line,
the crowd of runners bend forward,
fingers poised on wrists
to start their timers.
The air soundless until:
the gun goes off.

Now only the sound of countless
soles smacking pavement
as we run up Main Street
bunched until we turn the corner
heading up into the valley
before leaving the road
over gray shale gravel.

Then the real race starts
at the base of the mountain.
I veer off along the creek
and up a rock face
pulling myself up by alders
hanging over vertical sides
of a cleft in the cliff.

The trail slick with mud from last night's rain
disappears into ferns and devil's club.
Single file, I see nothing but bushes and butts.
I grab branches to keep from slipping
back into those behind me.
There is no passing here.
The adrenalin has worn off
and my calves want to cramp.
I'm drenched with sweat.

I break above the tree line
and a cold breeze hits me.
I can see the town of Seward
well below me. I'm halfway up now
where the leaders on their way down
from the top cross through us
skipping down the slope to our left.
I press my hands into my knees
to push myself uphill.

The trail steepest yet
I pull myself hand over hand
on the sharp rocks.
Next year I'll wear gloves.
I sing an infernal hymn to the peak:
Where the hell are you?
One damn false summit after another.

Finally, I break up over the edge
of the tundra plateau at the top.
I watch those ahead dissolve
in a cloudy mist that surrounds
the boulder and flag
at the back of the field.
A clammy cold soaks to the skin
as I make the turnaround
and head back down.

Over the edge, a relic snow drift
sits in a swale. Sliding is faster
than trying to run on the steep wet taiga.
A sharp shard of shale in the old snow
slices my left glute. When I stand
at the bottom of the drift,
blood runs down my leg.

The trail now broken bits of rock,
like running on a mattress.
My legs feel they can't
keep up with my body
and though the tops
of my shoes are taped,
they begin to fill with pebbles.

Crossing the up-trail, I careen
down a long narrow talus chute.
My feet slide three feet with each step.
It feels I'm falling until
I hit a rock outcrop hiding
just below the surface,
with a sudden jarring jerk
compressing my startled body.

Near the bottom of creek valley
I take a trail to left
avoiding cliffs ahead
which I leave to the experts.
At the end of side trail
I reach the short rock cliff
I climbed coming up
and swing down
onto the same alders
I had pulled myself higher.

Dropping down to the road
the pavement would feel a godsend
but my legs rebel
after sprinting straight up and down
and I run drunkenly a hundred yards.
My shoes chock full of rocks
feel like lead weights around my ankles.
I'm slogging hard,
trying to keep those behind behind.

I approach the finish line,
hearing the thumps of heavy shoes
following me. I can't let them pass
after all I've been through.
I want my body to sprint,
but it screams at me
and it's all I can do to ignore it.

In the finish area, I puke
and declare I will never do this again,
until next year when I do.

Coverings

Dad wore felt clogs
when walking dog Tina
to sooth tingling toes
from cholesterol-clogged arteries.
One night I woke to a call,
You'd better come to your father's house.
EMTs stood amid firetrucks
in small groups, talking lowly.
Mom said he was gone,
hugged me for the first time, then
recoiled realizing what she was doing.
He lay under a sheet
next to the dining room table.
His clogs peeked out from under,
yellow flowers against the grey.
We waited four hours for the coroner.
My younger brother kept lifting the sheet to see
Dad's thick tongue hanging out.
When they finally hauled him away
the clogs lay under the table for a year.
Mother gave them to me to wear
and with them passed her grief.
And with them I wore my grief.

Ways of Remembering

1.   Watching father pour liquid silver molten lead into a black sewer pipe joint before building the basement.

2.   He waking me with a jab, making sure my feet were on the floor, and tossing cold water on me if I fell back to sleep.

3.   Red buttocks after an angry spanking for throwing rocks through a neighbor's windows.

4.   Sitting in our car outside, waiting for Dad, at thirty below, while the warm garage was full of everything but a car.

5.   A Christmas present microscope with a culture of sea monkeys.

6.   His old Cadillac I never got to ride in.

7.   His messy workbench of dark greasy tools, though he wanted me to put the carpenter's crayon back exactly where I found it.

8.   His office, papers stacked on every surface with no place to work, though he was an excellent engineer and was proud when I too became an engineer.

9.   His years attempting to read lips because he would not admit he was deaf.

10.   Taking Ambien, his head hit the dining room table, spewing blood everywhere.

11.   A walking skeleton telling me just before his heart attack he didn't think he would be able to snow-blow the driveway next winter.

12.   Finding hidden trash bags stashed around the house because he couldn't ask for help.

13.   Hearing his voice again on his answering machine greeting.

Goodbye Mother

she fell in the night
broke her hip
before the operation
her gut impacted
coming out of the operation
the nurse asked
can I get you anything
"Yeah, how about a new husband"

after her hip operation
the infarction infected
I forgot she couldn't
make the connection
between her pain
and the morphine pump
when my sister
pushed the button
the wrinkles on my
mother's face smoothed
the pain undone

the doctor took us aside
we can't stop the infection
we couldn't avoid
the needed decision

they moved her to the death ward
drugged her so she wouldn't
feel her death
my siblings had to work
I spent the day with her
smoothed her bedclothes
in the evening twilight alpenglow
a harpist played

at four in the morning
I went home to rest
and wasn't with her when she died
so much left undone, so much unsaid

Lost Anchorage

The restored art deco theater
had a two-story 4th Avenue sign
suspended over its marque.
Built in '47, it made
the Register of Historic Places.
They tore it down.

It's lush lobby sported
red carpets, mirrored and mahogany walls
and a floor-to-ceiling mural
in gold and silver leaf of Mt. Denali.
They gutted it.

Two more gold and silver murals
flanked the movie screen
with pictures of gold miners, steamboats,
power houses and dogsleds.
They ripped them down.

The ceiling flickered with
the Big Dipper and the North Star
in a sky of velvet.
This they destroyed.

I watched *Journey to the Center of the Earth*
and as the actors descended
a vent in the volcano,
I hid behind the seats.
They tore them out too.

They also tore down
the grand staircase you climbed
with polished mahogany handrails
passing murals of foxes and flowers,
bear, caribou and dahl sheep.

I remember necking
with my high school sweetheart
in the darkened balcony
while watching *My Fair Lady*.
It's gone too.

And like my girlfriend,
they broke my heart the day it fell.
So, I will never enter the soulless building
that will replace that glorious theater.

Life

Dog Lichen lazing on the lawn,
belly to earth,
poised but relaxed,
a sphinx with a hidden riddle,
in sun-green shine,
stretch wriggles her paws
to me, asking no play
nothing to do or say,
only the moment
of connection
between us
as two beings
being.

Measures of Mortality

Momentary Birds

I watch workmates who, for gleeful sport,
rip sticks and mud from girders of a bridge,
dropping down to kick
puffed up nests perched on piers
into glacial torrents below.

Lobbing rocks, they chase the bobbing rafts of twigs.
Outstretched necks with baby beaks gaping as for food.
They laugh at tiny wings with frantic feathers
sinking beneath the cloudy water's sun-dumbing daze.

The scene takes me back
to my school bus stop,
when a friend strutted up
and bragged of shooting
chickadees with a thirty-ought-six.

Feathers floating to the ground.

On his own dare, he rode his horse
into the Chitina River.
The horse rolled in the raging silt
and came up empty-saddled.

Feathers floating down.

God of Ants

Back when I was just a little boy
I'd search the woods with my dog
to find bugs and other living toys.
I'd bust up some old and rotten log,

then take a stick to make the crazed ants run
this way and that and all around
to move their eggs to another dead stump
crawling through cranberry bushes on the ground.

One day I decided to stage a tragic act.
Taking an old and rusted tin can, I chose
for actors one red ant and another black
and tried to make them fight in close.

I thought to play god from above,
but the ants just ignored my love.

What Had I Done?

Wanting the forbidden
I whacked the flying dragonfly
with a baseball bat.
Silence lay like a mausoleum
in bright sunlight.
I held the dead bug
and stared at what I had done.
Perfectly preserved
the hooked tail
the translucent gasoline tinted wings
that no more would fly.
And losing my childhood fascination
I pitched it in the bushes.
Misplacing my essence
I had slain the messenger.

Man Bear

we gorged on watermelon that night
the red juice running down our cheeks
tossing the rinds in the latrine
later we were wakened by our elders
and told to stay in our tents
so as not to see
what was being done
and of course we peeked
through the boreal summer's midnight twilight
to see the terrified animal
surrounded by our men betters
standing on its hind legs
as the shot pierced its bared chest
and it screamed like a man

Black Bear Sow

She presented herself
with cubs through
spruce and birch,
choosing not to bolt
like other bears
that spotted me.
Instead, she seemed content
to let me stand
watering my morning lawn
as she towed the two
toward me.
She brought them
over the hose
between my spraying
and the blaring pump
down by the pond.
She shooed her brood
up a cottonwood.
They scrambled branchless, up
the rough bark until after
resting on the first thick branch,
they climbed to the top
swaying in the thin breeze
before sliding down the trunk
then climbing in the air again and again.
When I went in,
she brought them down
and took them up the mountain.

The hiker told the reporter later
she had charged him
and he had to shoot her.

A Dog Named Lichen

She no longer leaped
to her doghouse rooftop,
or dashed down to the pond.
No more hopping the garden fence,
digging up carrots and devouring them.

To stand in her icy pen—
an epic struggle.

We laid her on the warm kitchen floor.

Beneath her eyes lacking clarity
I could still see the mystery of who she was.

Why her locked leg bumped the stove
as the needle went in,
I wondered, as I noted
the nothing now behind her eyes.

Scott's Pond

We watched a bull moose
on our lawn for two weeks
barely changing position
as it stood lifting one front leg
and then the other
when not lying down
sleeping, its head propped on
one antler, floating above the frost
frozen grass.

A cow moose and later another
bull entered the lawn's sphere
but our moose would not entertain
any notion of recognition.

The third week, it slowly moseyed
down to the pond,
named for a dead boy,
broke ice with its hoof
and drank water.

Two more weeks passed
of wandering around our house
when it withdrew behind
a stand of trees by the pond
and died as skaters skated around
its frozen faintly reeking carcass
as wind waved through the alders
chiming the ice rimed branches.

Ravens and magpies pecked out its eyes
and chased a coyote back across the pond
and hassled a young bald eagle,
but did not deter bears
we could not see behind trees
as they snuck through the woods
on a well pawed trail in the snow
and tore the bones apart
and hauled them away.

Now nothing is left except
two ribs and some fur.

Nature's Ways

Bit tulips lie clipped,
fresh dead, no decay,
a hare had bit,
before humans could pick.
But up the mountainside,

no moose, no hare,
disturbs alpine blooms:
elfin shooting star,
ruminating monkshood,

squat dwarf violet,
and placid glacial avens,
on a high-clouded peak
that stands in its own presence.

Halfway Round Two-Day Trail

Through the backcountry of Crow Pass
past Raven Glacier
across the boulder piles
and over gorge's bridge
nothing human for miles and miles
plunging through waist-high grass that
hid my tripping feet.
An electric pain stings
from bees between sweaty thighs.

And I see a grizzly lumber
onto the trail fifty yards ahead.

*Don't run. Don't
run. The bear would chase.*

Fight or play dead?

Backing down the trail
and stepping behind
a short scrawny spruce—
*if he wants me, this tree provides
no protection.*

Dropping my pack from my back,
fishing for pepper spray, I fumble,
knocking the cannister out
onto the trail on a miss-grab—
too close, no time
to retrieve, my
only defense
gone.

Muscles ripple under
tawny fur. Long sharp
claws ripping my
imagined face. I smell
the stench
of his breath.

Then the wet black bulging nose passes.
ignoring my presence, wanting only
the right-of-way,
taking it on down the trail.

And as he leaves,
I feel again my inner thigh
with its prayerful pain.

Descending Near Peak's Southern Slope

After hiking the afternoon
two ravens circle above me.
They are met by many more
nearly fifty, gamboling,
gyring ever higher,
dipping, falling back towards earth
calling to each other
with glugging clucking water music.

At first I think it's me
they choose to play above,
and move me with their motion,
but no: only the rising
thermals of the sun lift them up.
And when they tire of their play
they continue home beyond the peak
and I on down the mountainside.

Upon a Day, Came Sorrow In To Me—Dante Alighieri

Post-Polio

As a child, polio paralyzed
an arm and both legs.
Months of excruciating exercises
reattached motor neurons to her muscles,
one neuron adopting the work of fifteen others.
She learned to run and relished the training
to win marathons before women
were supposed to race that distance.

She didn't know why her times kept dropping
and runners beat her as never before
and her toes drooped when lifting her foot.
The doctor said it was post-polio.
They thought she should repeat
the same exercises as a child,
but didn't realize the exercises
killed her remaining neurons—
she needed rest instead.
But for their exercises
and if she had stopped running,
she would have had a normal life.

Instead, she only had strength
to walk a few steps before
she needed to rest for hours.
She wore braces to stop her toes from sagging
and employed a power chair to move about.
We fitted the house with ramps outside,
and a stair-lift inside to carry her from floor to floor.

She told me it all was just
another form of training.

You

But all we know are fragments of the world.
    —William Bronk

We come into this world knowing little:
Only a plasma cloud of possibility
And we try to learn the *isness* of *is*.
Our brain tries to make sense
of the dancing points of light
from the firehose of sense data
pushing us back toward unknowing
as we fight for fragments of knowing
we piece together shards of fractured mirrors
to dream the reality we think around us.

So, I can't truly know what it is to be you.
Are your qualia my qualia; your red, my red?
I can only hope my valentine
looks the same to you as me.
Since I have created you to me
from fragments of you that you gave to me
all the time up until you weren't.
It's a wonder I could know
anything of you at all.

Leukemia

Just cremated dog Willow's
cancer bitten bones,
and drove my wife Gail
to her annual exam,
my back spasming,

my mind misplaced. Post-polio
did not let her drive. I lay in agony
on the lobby floor as doctors
poked and prodded Gail.

Later that day, they called her back.
The tests looked
wrong, white
cell count way too high.
She joked when I asked the new results.

She hid them from me
until sitting on the bed, she calmly said:
leukemia. I realized then that
she hadn't wanted me worrying about her
while I drove in intense pain.

Right. They cured my cousin of that cancer.
It took them two weeks to decide
there was no cure for Gail's. *Can you be in
Seattle in the morning?*

They killed her blood cells.
The pieces clogged her kidneys
and almost killed her. I slept
beside her for a month on pain
pills before they let us fly home.

She searched the web before
the doctor would say.
Two years, I read hoping . . .
No, she corrected, only one.

I pumped care and saline into her port
each day to keep her arteries clear
for chemo at the oncology ward
where all waited dying.
She kept her dark brown hair
and looked so good
the doctor would forget
and she kindly reminded him
she was too old for
a stem cell exchange.

Then came the day the doctor sat me down.
If there's anything you need to do: do it!
Turns out she had known to the day
when she would die.

Our pastor never asked
about her cancer. She simply told him:
three months. Delivering her eulogy
He called her by some other woman's name.
Such details about herself
wouldn't have mattered to her.

I cry when I hear the hymns
she picked for her memorial service.

True Beauty

When my wife died
in her hospital bed we placed in the living room,
looking out on the pond, Wallace Stevens'
words came to mind:
"Death is the mother of Beauty."
I remembered her face that day, and wondered
if *this* was the beauty he was thinking of.
I don't really think so. Then there's Keats':
"Truth is beauty, beauty truth." It then follows
that Stevens' words become "Death is the
mother of truth" And yes, she is truly
dead, and I must remain alive to face Stevens'
lonely fact that death makes
life beautiful, even her death.
And then I kissed her lips.

Clinched Viscera

The moon enlightens
Two long thin white clouds above
Brightly sparkling snow

Clouds

The day's necessities
hid her leukemia and

would not show her dying.
Others could not see.

She moved behind
a vaporous glass reflecting

my grief back on me
and so it did not show.

She a shade moving
through her own reality,

her only care to be a cloud
to time past:

the cirrus of remembering
now caught on

clouded pane. And trying
to wipe it clean she

waited to be free
of what others thought of her.

Musings

silence is one part of knowing
sitting with the spirit of dearest memory
feeling its gravity condense from mirage
cast from the fragrance of night

I Will Never Know Another You

You said you had passed your expiration date.
You picked hymns and poems and didn't tell me.

You said after many hospice signatures:
You have to fill out paperwork even to die.

You never complained of your post-polio syndrome.
You never complained about your cancer.

You dressed yourself two days before you died.
You said nothing of the pain, but when the meds were right

Your face said you were finally at peace.

All the Chairs

Log rockers on the west deck
look out on an alder-strewn draw.

Blue loungers on the east deck
gaze over the pond.

To the north a park bench weathered and worn
searches the Chugach Mountain tops.

By the garden, smooth orange metal chairs
relax from weeding in the afternoon sun.

Back on the lawn, black metal seats
quietly convene.

Down at the pond a short-legged bench
watches mallards and teals.

Post-polio let her walk from one
to the other. She then had to rest.

Then came the cancer:
the chairs rest empty.

Composting

I just turned her bins, as I've done every fall.
  Three: three by three and three feet high,
stand aslant with age, and held by brass screws,
  The grey notched boards with gaps between.
The first held pieces of vegetable leavings,
  grass clippings, dog feces and dead leaves,
with memories of our separate lives.
  The bottom a fetid gelatinous slithering mass of earthworms.

Visited by winter white ermine and a bear,
  with lichen-laced cedar and bright blond mold,
a cold green fire burns and worms
  persist in their pursuit of dead matter.
In the second bin, decomposing and merging morsels
  continue, converting death into life.
These piles followed her from home to home
  for twenty years before I came to help.

In the last bin all is done. Brown peaty soil
  now with no smell, each shovelful brimming with life.
Fully merged, death now for the living, the soil composed,
  our lives fully mingled. It is finished.
The nutrients are for garden and lawn, new grass,
  broccoli, carrots, lettuce and peas.
These piles where so much a part of her life that when she
  was gone, her daughter listed them as the last of her survivors.

Requiem

For my wife

Do you remember the night our tallest cottonwood blew down?
And how the wind howled so loud we didn't hear it fall?
At dawn, the stately trunk stretched from the pond
to our lawn. The shattered stump stood mute
as we sawed and chopped the limbs free, leaving
the gray gnarled bark log lying on the ground.
We imagined the tree had loved
the wind and the wind had loved it back.

Remember the eagles perching and watching tasty baby mallards
from its branches, and how tuft-headed kingfishers
dove down for silver Dolly Varden fingerlings.
And clouds of chickadees, swallows or pine siskins
hid in its leaves. We saw a sow chase her bumbly cubs
to the top. Down one slid till stopped suddenly by its largest limb.

Center now rotten, outer wood awaits,
pierced by beetles and ants,
by sprouts of its own roots.
I too will change form and follow
the tree, the wind, and you.

Afterlife

after Bruce Snider

I wake to untrimmed branches reaching out
to close the driveway. Her trimmer still

hangs on her scooter basket, sharp.
I choose books from those she chose

for the Little Free Library she asked me to
build on the snow. Later I sank a permanent post

after spring breakup thawed frost.
The willow grows green up to the red door

she painted. I take her clipper
to clear the twigs around the box.

They still come to swap books.

Bones

winter wind blows down
from Wolverine's mountainside
stripping birched ridges

leaving treetops bare of frost
lower branches flashing light

a first skim of snow
covers winter-wooded paths
dead roots of live trees

still show through gray against white
marking trails we used to take

Dog Dish Rock

There's a trail on the mountain
I hiked as a boy. Now
the house sits next to it.
On the way up, our dogs leaped up
and lapped rainwater from a bowl
atop a boulder midst berries blue and crow.
We picked there often
and she asked that her ashes
be spread below the rock.
I put down dog Lupine
two weeks after she passed.
Both their ashes lie there now. So
I stop on the way up
with new dog Daisy who too drinks
rainwater from Dog Dish Rock.

Renewal

Lethe

You and I met on the shadowed span
Over the lyrical river
Climbed the arduous path
Towards morning light.
I turned, reached out,
And you were gone.

Ode to Odds

Chances are charming   come change the game.
Odds offer opportunity   but outcomes may fail.
Though usually you lose   sometimes you win.
Fortune affects results   rams in the real,
sword swinger of is   the scythe of risk,
the winner's way   and the loser's woe.
Einstein declared God   didn't play dice
but Bohr wouldn't tell   what God should do.
God didn't say what would be   just there would be.
In due time we die   but death's worth the ride.
You've already achieved.   All is here.
Put down your bets   and take your fate.

High Latitude

Low-hanging orange orb, just above the lone and faraway horizon
brings back a longing for what might have been

and recalls the old fear for what the world will offer without her.
Stand against the light and try to be what you should.

For it all comes rushing in, crushing the gut. Why can't there be
more yellow? Orange should not survive.

When the sun does yellow out of darkness, reminding of what is and was:
cold, cold life that curdles future. I do not want to be here.

She is gone.

Time Scales

A narrow two-lane road
winding down into the valley
was widened into a highway
by cutting into the tall bluff
exposing its soil profile
at the angle of repose.
Alternating layers
of silts, sands, gravels,
dotted with cobbles and boulders,
patiently suffered
rinsing summer rains,
heaving winter frosts,
and the downhill creep of thawing soils.
The lowest layers displayed
many millions of years
and Cretaceous fossil
ammonites protruded
from salty clay and siltstone.

How long since the explosive
birth of the universe
did these creatures appear?
And how long until
the sun explodes
engulfing the earth
and the universe collapses
back into a singular
bit of all existence?

There is No Consolation in the Thought of God
A Cento

I have lived enough not to believe in heaven,
but in sunlight uncompromised
by God, or lack of God,
and am confounded by God.
I have no fear of God but of being.
To live in nature is to suffer luck
and live by meanings I cannot comprehend,
in the Lord's emptiness
in whose image we are made,
I live in a world I never understand.
My incantations conjure the form of the world,
my flesh but a fresh-embroidered shroud.

With thanks to Christian Wiman twice, Jericho Brown twice, Kazeem Ali,
Osip Mandelstam twice, Ilya Kaminsky, William Bronk twice, Elinor Wylie.

Latent Dreams

After Basho translated by Jane Hirschfield

Do we wish to wake to the
image of a curved crescent
beach illuminated by moon
light reflected on waves giving it
the appearance of truth but also
a whispering world resembling
the unknown emptiness of nothing?

Solstice

The smothering cold darkness closes in again.
Later inside, I look out my window
at the first early light this year:
new season peeking from behind dark mountains,
and the eternal light that had flashed
from the beginning, is new once more.

Fibonacci

sink
down
into
acceptance
and feel deep relief
flowing through your sorrowful soul

The Weight of Light

Light like grace
falls with humility,
reflecting everywhere
at once upon the pond
and moving with us
as we change our view,
offering us a new perspective:
sun on wren and iris,
covering too, a cruelly bared body
with the seamless linen shroud
of imagination, creating reality
from the response of our mind.

Mine Among Hers 55

Succulent jade leaves
Grow from a white coffee cup
Stamped with red hearts.
Does it need a larger pot
To set its bound-up roots free?

The Birch

An aged tree stood
at the side of the road.
Fist-sized stones ringed
its roots, rosary beads.
White tattered paper bark fluttered
in the breeze, frayed crepe
from a long past fête.
One black branch pointed
to where I'd been, another
to where I was going.
The trunk stood straight
in place, north side
sheathed in golden lichen, as if
the sun had set that way.
A scar showed grey dead
wood from some past attack.
And above the wound
a worried crack after
some tempestuous storm, ran
up the trunk, revealing
vivid wood to the core.
Still it grew passing tall, branches
sporting glorious green effusions.
I left it standing beside the road
yearning it would endure.

Goes On

after Billy Collins

There are times when *to be* is a curse.
I lose your keys in the house
and waste hours looking for them.
The 4Runner's battery is dead
and I miss your urologist appointment.
The washer decides to leak,
flooding the floor.
It can't get any worse when
the rattle in her throat
becomes mute.

Winter plays tricks with my mind.
She still sleeps by my side.
The house doesn't care now
that I wish it was a monastery.
It provides no rest.
I seek life in others
but they couldn't know.

Come spring I work in the garden
turning the soil.
The black earth beckons
with each shovelful.
Earthworms and beetles
roam through the loam.
Shoots push upwards
despite my despair.

The third year a sunflower
breaks through.
Another *she* enters the garden.
Life comes anew.
There is someone now
who understands.

Middle Fork

I stand above misted trees that cling
to cliffs that shine from the gorge
with a powerful peace. A muffled rumble
calls from the unseen stream, spirit of
an unsunned shadow under leaves. Earth's stony
gash below my feet, an oracle,
nothing to mankind. It is earth's breath,
today ignored. Yet its jealous
grasping tears at the heart
amid blood-red salmon berries.
The silent swoop of a great horned owl
floats over the chasm,
a quiet ghost with extended
claws, gray feathers aflutter in its
wind. Flight mastered
without demand but to the depths below
where waits the unsuspecting hare.
There will come a time when
I step down and count myself
a part of this and join
the god talk of the gorge.

Acknowledgments

I am grateful to the editors of *Cirque Literary Journal* for publishing earlier versions of "Momentary Birds," "Dog Dish Rock," "Baxter Bog, 1955," "Afterlife" and "Running Mount Marathon." I am also grateful to the editors of *100 Fresh Alaskan Poems*, 2026, for publishing earlier versions of "God of Ants," "What Have I Done," "Man Bear," "Black Bear Sow," "Human Purposes," "Nature's Ways," "Halfway Around Two-Day Trail," "Scott's Pond," "Descending Near Peak's Southern Slope," and "Middle Fork."

I would like to thank my wife, Marilyn Lee, for her patience and support during the many hours I spent away from her working on my manuscript; the monthly poetry reading group, Poetry Parley, that provided me with a group of peers that has given me invaluable experience in reading these poems in public; and my weekly writing group, Drumlins, that provided much needed feedback on my writing and especially Vivian Faith Prescott who mentors us. I thank my peers in the University of Alaska Anchorage poetry program for providing their insights on my poems. I also thank all the UAA Creative Writing and Literary Arts faculty for rounding out my writing experience. I want to thank my mentors: Anne Caston, who showed me new possibilities for my poetry; Ishmael Hope, who provided me with a solid background in philosophical poetry as well as the oral poetry tradition; and Erin Coughlin Hollowell, my thesis advisor and editor. I also thank Mike Burwell, editor of *Cirque Literary Journal* and Peggy Schumaker, editor of the University of Alaska Press for their insightful comments on my poems. I especially want to thank Zack Rogow for helping me edit my poems and assemble my manuscript.

About the Author

Eric Gordon Johnson was born in Fairbanks in 1948 and raised in Anchorage, Alaska. He is a retired geotechnical engineer, a mountain runner, a cross-country skier, a clarinet player and a tenor. He sings in the Anchorage Concert Chorus and the Anchorage Opera Chorus. He and his wife live adjacent to Chugach State Park on the mountains above Anchorage. He earned an MFA in Creative Writing in poetry at the University of Alaska, Anchorage in December of 2020. He has published poetry, fiction and memoir in *Cirque Literary Journal, Alaska Humanities Forum, Anchorage Daily News and Anchorage Remembers.* He is a member of Drumlin Poets, Poetry Parley and 49Writers. He has also taught poetry classes for Opportunities for Lifelong Education.

About Cirque Press

Cirque Press grew out of *Cirque*, a literary journal that publishes the works of writers and artists from the North Pacific Rim, a region that reaches north from Oregon to the Yukon Territory, south through Alaska to Hawaii, and west to the Russian Far East.

Cirque Press is a partnership of Sandra Kleven, publisher, and Michael Burwell, editor. Ten years ago, we recognized that works of talented writers in the region were going unpublished, and the Press was launched to bring those works to fruition. We publish fiction, nonfiction, and poetry, and we seek to produce art that provides a deeper understanding about the region and its cultures. The writing of our authors is significant, personal, and strong.

Sandra Kleven – Michael Burwell, publishers and editors

www.cirquejournal.com

Poetry from Cirque Press

Apportioning the Light by Karen Tschannen (2018)

The Lure of Impermanence by Carey Taylor (2018)

Echolocation by Kristin Berger (2018)

Like Painted Kites & Collected Works by Clifton Bates (2019)

Athabaskan Fractal: Poems of the Far North
    by Karla Linn Merrifield (2019)

Holy Ghost Town by Tim Sherry (2019)

Silty Water People by Vivian Faith Prescott (2020)

The Dream That Is Childhood by Sandra Wassilie (2020)

Lily Is Leaving: Poems by Leslie Ann Fried (2021)

November Reconsidered by Marc Janssen (2021)

Callie Comes of Age by Dale Champlin (2021)

Fish the Dead Water Hard by Eric Heyne (2021)

Salt & Roses by Buffy McKay (2022)

Growing Older In This Place: A Life in Alaska's Rainforest
    by Margo Wasserman Waring (2022)

On the Beach: Poems 2016-2021 by Alan Weltzien (2022)

Between Promise and Sadness by Joanne Townsend (2022)

Yosemite Dawning by Shauna Potocky (2022)

The Woman Within
    by Tami Phelps and Kerry Dean Feldman (2023)

Getting Home from Here by Anne Ward-Masterson (2023)

Crossing the Burnside Bridge & Other Poems
    by Janice D. Rubin (2023)

A Variable Sense of Things by Ron McFarland (2023)

If Singing Went On by Gerald Cable (2024)

Bury Me in Cherry Blossoms by Eric Braman (2024)

Last Call of the Dark by Mary Eliza Crane (2024)

The Nancy Poems by John Morgan (2024)

Into the Khumbu by Alan Weltzien (2025)

Dancing Away by Robert M. Fagen (2025)

Sea Smoke, Spindrift and Other Spells by Shauna Potocky (2025)

Lost Last Poems by Shannon Gramse (2025)

Give Me an Endless Range by John Baalke (2025)

Forced Landing by David McElroy (2025)

God Talk of the Gorge by Eric Gordon Johnson (2026)